Oxford**basics**

Presenting
New Language

Oxford basics

Presenting
New Language

Jill Hadfield
Charles Hadfield

OXFORD

UNIVERSITY PRESS

Oxford University Press
Great Clarendon Street, Oxford OX2 6DP

Oxford New York
Athens Auckland Bangkok Bogotá
Buenos Aires Calcutta Cape Town Chennai
Dar es Salaam Delhi Florence Hong Kong
Istanbul Karachi Kuala Lumpur Madrid
Melbourne Mexico City Mumbai Nairobi
Paris São Paulo Singapore Taipei Tokyo
Toronto Warsaw

and associated companies in
Berlin Ibadan

OXFORD and OXFORD ENGLISH
are trade marks of Oxford University Press

ISBN 0 19 442167 8

Typeset by Mike Brain Graphic Design Limited,
Oxford

Printed in Hong Kong

Contents

Foreword

There is a formidable range of materials published worldwide for teachers of English as a Foreign Language. However, many of these materials, especially those published in English-speaking countries, assume that the teachers using them will be working with smallish classes and have abundant resources available to them. Also many, if not most, of these materials make implicit culturally-biased assumptions about the beliefs and values of the teachers and learners.

This situation is ironic in view of the fact that the vast majority of English as a Foreign Language classrooms do not correspond at all to these conditions. Typically, classes are large, resources are limited, and teachers have very few opportunities for training and professional development. Also, the cultural assumptions of teachers and learners in many parts of the world may vary quite significantly from those of materials writers and publishers.

This book is an attempt to address this situation. The authors present 30 lessons at elementary level, each with the same methodological framework. The lessons are explained in clear, accessible language, and none of them require sophisticated resources. Instead, they call on the basic human resources which all teachers and learners bring with them to class. The language points covered are ones found in a typical elementary course, and the topics are those which form part of everybody's daily lives, for example families, homes, and leisure activities.

Most importantly, however, the book offers a framework for teachers who lack training and support. The hope and the expectation is that such teachers will begin by following each step of a lesson quite closely but, as their confidence increases, will adapt and add to the techniques presented here, responding to the particular needs and abilities of their learners.

This is an important book: one of the few attempts to address the problems of the 'silent majority' of teachers worldwide who have little or no training, and few resources to work with.

ALAN MALEY
Assumption University
Bangkok, Thailand

Introduction

English is taught all over the world, by all sorts of teachers to all sorts of learners. Schools and classrooms vary enormously in their wealth and their provision of equipment. Learners are very different from place to place. But, whatever the conditions in which you are working, there is one resource which is universal and unlimited: the human mind and imagination. This is probably the one single most valuable teaching and learning resource we have. Nothing can replace it. In even the most 'hi-tech' environment, a lack of imagination and humanity will make the most up-to-date and sophisticated resources seem dull; conversely, the most simple resources can be the most exciting and useful.

We have been fortunate to spend quite a lot of our time working not only in 'hi-tech' environments with computers and video, but also in classrooms where there is little more than blackboard and chalk and some out-of-date coursebooks. Some of our most interesting learning and teaching experiences (as Confucius said, a teacher is 'always ready to teach; always ready to learn') have been not in the comfortable well-resourced small classrooms of a private language school, but in classrooms where only the minimum of equipment has been available. Equally, some of our most memorable teaching experiences in 'hi-tech' classrooms have been when we have abandoned the cassette or video or glossy coursebook and got to work with that most precious resource of all, the learners' own experience and imagination.

Teachers often have to use materials which are out of date, or contain subject-matter irrelevant to their particular group of learners. For example, we have had great difficulty explaining the concepts of the fridge-freezer and microwave oven to Tibetans. In the same way, learners who have spent all their lives in northern countries might have difficulty with an exercise from an African textbook which asks if they prefer yam or cassava. So over the last few years we have been trying to design materials which can be used in as wide a range of teaching situations as possible.

The activities we suggest are as flexible as the human imagination is creative; they are 'teacher resource material' which teachers will be able to adjust to suit their particular environment. In thinking about universally applicable, 'lo-tech' materials we have come up with a list of criteria that need to be met. The materials will need to:

- be usable in large classes as well as small.
- be suitable for adult learners as well as secondary learners, and if possible easily adaptable to a primary context.
- be centered on the universals of human experience.

- cover the main language skills and have a useful base of grammar and topic vocabulary.
- be traditional enough to be recognizable by all teachers, and thus give them a sense of security, while providing communicative activities for learners.
- be non-threatening in the demands they make on learners.
- be teacher-based 'resource material' rather than books for learners.
- assume that no technical and reprographic resources are available and be based on the human resource rather than the technical.
- be culturally neutral, not context-bound, and thus be flexible, easily adaptable by the teachers to their own culture and teaching context.
- be flexible enough to complement a standard syllabus or coursebook.

Presenting New Language

This book contains thirty activities, designed according to the criteria above, for presenting new language at elementary level. When you are presenting new language, you need to do three things:

- **Create a context** for the new language. In other words, you need to show the learners how the language is used and what it means.
- **Focus on the form** of the new language in order to help the learners remember it and relate it to language they already know.
- **Check comprehension**—it is important to check that the learners have understood how to form and use the new language.

All the activities in this book are divided into stages which correspond to these three needs.

Creating a context

The new language should be presented in a context that makes its meaning clear. In a textbook this is done for you, for example by means of a reading or listening text, or a set of pictures. But if you have no coursebook, or want to use an activity in this book instead of your coursebook, you will need to create a context yourself. Each of the activities contains suggestions to help you, for example simple texts you can use or adapt, and pictures you can copy. You can also make use of the classroom furniture, and even the learners themselves!

Texts

Some of the activities include a simple dialogue, or a description or story. In each case, a basic text is provided for you, but it is best if you adapt it to suit your teaching situation and the learners you are working with. For example in 16 'Rooms in a flat', there is a description of a plan of a flat, but you may want to adapt this if your school is in a small town or village and most of your learners live in houses.

When you are using a text, try not to read it out—it will be more effective if you try to speak more naturally, partly from memory. This will involve some preparation. First read the text, then write down the main points in note form. For the text in 24 'Daily routines' for example, your notes might look like this:

get up—wash—have breakfast—brush my teeth—walk to school —have lunch—go home—cook supper—watch TV—go to bed

Practise speaking the text on your own, using just the notes to help you, until you feel confident to use it with your class.

Pictures

Pictures may be drawn on the board, on large pieces of paper ('posters'), or on pieces of card ('flashcards'). Sometimes one kind of picture is more appropriate than another. A set of vocabulary items, for example food or clothes, are best drawn on a set of flashcards which can be held up one at a time so that the learners are not confused by too much new vocabulary at once. Make sure that the flashcards are big enough to be seen at the back of the class, but not too big to be handled easily. A more complex picture needs to be drawn on the board or on a poster. Posters have obvious advantages over drawings on the board: you can prepare them in advance and they can be stored and used again. Try to find a cheap source of large sheets of paper for posters. In Madagascar, for example, the teachers we worked with found the sheets of paper used for wrapping vegetables in the market were ideal for making posters. A good way to fix posters or flashcards to the board is to pin a length of string along the top of the board like a clothes-line. You can then use clothes-pegs to peg your posters to the string!

If you feel you can't draw, don't worry. When pictures are needed in an activity, simple drawings are provided for you to copy.

Realia

Real objects or 'realia' can be used as an alternative to drawings. Activities like 20 'In the market' and 21 'Shopping' are more interesting for the learners if you use real food and drink.

Mime

Another way to create a context is to use mime. You don't have to be an actor or actress—the mimes in these activities are all very simple everyday actions such as brushing your teeth or opening a door. It is a good idea to practise the mimes before you do them in front of the class. If possible, try to do the action in reality first, for example open a real door. What movements are involved? Now try making the movements without the real object—open an imaginary door. Repeat this in front of a mirror. Are there any improvements you could make to try to make the mime clearer? Practising in this way will give you the confidence use the mimes in front of your class.

Visualization

This means asking learners to close their eyes and imagine a scene. You can prompt them with questions as they do this, for example:

> Close your eyes. I want you to think of your family. What are they doing now? Think of your mother … Where is she? … What is she doing? Don't answer, just imagine … Now your father …

It is important to tell the learners that they don't have to respond to the questions in words, only in mental pictures. Talk slowly and gently, giving the learners plenty of time to think. Because everyone imagines a different scene, this way of creating a context gives the learners plenty of opportunity for real communication as they describe 'their' scene.

Focus on form

After the meaning of the new language has been established, you will want to show the learners how it is formed. All the techniques here use visual presentation, which is usually easier for students to understand than verbal explanation. One way of showing visually how the various parts of language fit together is the substitution table, for example:

I'd like	one	bottle/s	please.
	two	packet/s	
	three	tin/s	

You can turn a list of vocabulary into a simple substitution table by adding words, for example:

> *father*
>
> *mother*
>
> *husband*

can become:

This is my   *father*

               mother

               husband

Remember to leave space on the board for the extra words.

Another useful variation if you want the learners to practise a dialogue is speech bubbles:

> *Where's the cinema?*

> *It's opposite the restaurant.*

You can draw attention to important points by highlighting them in coloured chalks or pen, for example the stressed words in a dialogue:

Hello. My name's Ben. What's your name?

My name's Kate. Nice to meet you.

You can even use learners as visual aids by writing words on large labels and pinning them to their backs. The learners then arrange themselves in diffferent ways to make sentences. You can find an example of this technique in 4 'Telling the time'.

Checking comprehension

In order to check that learners have understood how the language is used and how it is formed, you need to give them an opportunity to use it for themselves. This allows you to check understanding and prepare the way for further practice. It also gives learners confidence in handling the new language.

Checking comprehension can be done in several ways. It is important to start with techniques that involve the whole class, for example:

- 'Teacher–learner', where the teacher asks questions and the learners answer, or the learners ask questions and the teacher answers.
- 'Half-class–half-class', where half the class ask questions in chorus and the other half reply.
- 'Open pairs', where two learners ask and answer while the rest listen.

This is the stage at which you can check if students are using the target language correctly and confidently before proceeding to practise in 'closed pairs' (where the whole class are working in pairs at the same time), or small groups. You can find out if there are any problems and can clear up misunderstandings. If there is a real muddle you may even decide to go back to the 'Creating a context' or the 'Focus on form' stage.

Pronunciation points

Each activity contains suggestions for pronunciation work. The pronunciation points dealt with arise directly out of the language being presented in the activity. While it is impossible to address every problem that users of the book will encounter, we have made an attempt to cover points that many learners will find troublesome, like stress patterns, intonation in different types of question and statement, and some work on individual sounds, focusing on those that give trouble most often such as long and short vowels, and the /θ/ sound. Suggestions for teaching the learners to produce individual sounds are given in each activity. In general, a useful technique is to get the learners to produce and practise the sound in isolation first, then go on to produce it in a word, and then to produce the word in a sentence.

Stress

There are various techniques for practising stress patterns, both in individual words and in sentences, for example:

- Get the learners to clap out the rhythm before saying the word or sentence.
- Get the learners to tap out the rhythm on their desks as they repeat the sentence.
- Dictate the word or sentence and get the learners to mark the stress.

Intonation

The main patterns dealt with are:

- Falling intonation in question-word questions, for example:

   Where's the station?

- Rising intonation in yes/no questions, for example:

   Do you like fish?

- Falling intonation in answers and negative statements, for example:

   No, there isn't any sugar.

- Falling intonation in commands, for example:

   You mustn't smoke.

There are various techniques for practising intonation patterns, for example:

- Show with hand movements how the voice rises or falls.
- Get the learners to make appropriate hand movements up or down as they repeat the sentences.
- Get the learners to mirror the rise or fall physically, for example when they repeat a yes/no question get them to begin the question in a seated position and to stand up as their voice rises at the end of the sentence.
- Dictate the sentence and get the learners to mark the intonation arrows up or down.

Building a lesson

There are two companion books to this one, *Simple Listening Activities* and *Simple Speaking Activities*. Each of these also contains thirty activities, and in all three books the topics and the language presented and practised correspond. So, for example, activity 1 in all three books is about 'Greetings and introductions' and activity 30 is about 'Describing actions'. The activities in each book are graded, following a basic structural syllabus. This means that you can design your own lesson or sequence of lessons using material from one, two, or all three books, depending on your learners' needs and the time available.

Activities

1 Greetings and introductions

NEW LANGUAGE	Hello. My name's _____. What's your name? Nice to meet you.
REVISION	None.
MATERIALS	The dialogue below; the pictures below on two posters, or on the board.
PREPARATION	Copy the pictures; prepare the dialogue.
TIME GUIDE	30 minutes.

Creating a context
   1 Show the learners these pictures. Ask them, in their own language, what they think is happening.

2 Read this dialogue to the class, using different voices for Ben and Kate. Point to Ben when he is speaking, and to Kate when she is speaking.

BEN   Hello. My name's Ben. What's your name?
KATE My name's Kate. Nice to meet you.
BEN   Nice to meet you too.

Checking comprehension 3 Ask a volunteer to come to the front and repeat the dialogue with you. This time, use your and the learner's real names. Remodel the learner's answers if necessary, for example:

TEACHER *Hello. My name's _____. What's your name?*
LEARNER *My name _____.*
TEACHER [quietly] *'My name's _____.'*
LEARNER *My name's _____. Nice to meet you.*
TEACHER *Nice to meet you too.*

4 Walk around the class introducing yourself to different learners, repeating the dialogue each time.

Focus on form

5   If the pictures are on the board, write in the dialogue. If you are using posters, put up the second poster.

6   Divide the class in half down the middle. Tell one half 'You are Ben' and the other half 'You are Kate'. Get the class to repeat the dialogue after you, one half of the class repeating Ben's part and the other half repeating Kate's. When they are confident, get them to switch parts. If necessary, work on pronunciation at this stage.

7   Then get the learners to practise the dialogue in pairs. First get them to work with the learner sitting next to them, then with the learner sitting in front of or behind them.

Pronunciation points

■   Practise the stress patterns in the dialogue:

Hello. My name's Ben. What's your name?

My name's Kate. Nice to meet you.

Nice to meet you too.

■   Practise falling intonation in question-word questions:

What's your name?

2 The alphabet

NEW LANGUAGE	The letters of the alphabet.
REVISION	None.
MATERIALS	The 'Alphabet song'; if possible, a guitar or other musical instrument.
PREPARATION	Practise the song.
TIME GUIDE	30 minutes.

Focus on form

1   Write the alphabet in its usual sequence on the left-hand side of the board. On the right-hand side, write the letters in sound groups (see 'Pronunciation points').

A B C D E F G   A H J K
H I J K L M N   B C D E G P T V
O P Q R S T U   F L M N S X Z
V W X Y Z   I Y
                          O
                          Q U W
                          R

2   Get the class to repeat the letters in sound groups after you. Then ask individual learners to repeat one or two sound groups each.

3   Get the class to repeat the alphabet in its usual sequence.

Creating a context

4   Teach the 'Alphabet song'.

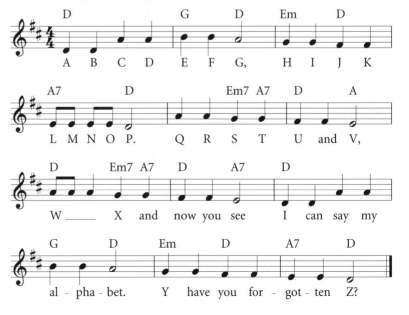

12

Checking comprehension **5** Point to letters in random order and get the learners to repeat them.

6 Call out individual learners' initials and get the class to identify the learner, for example:

TEACHER *A. M. Who is it?*
LEARNERS *Anna Marks!*
TEACHER *Yes. That's right!*

7 Get the learners to do both the calling out and the guessing. The learner who guesses correctly can call out the next set of initials each time.

Pronunciation points ◾ The phonemes for the sound groups are as follows:

A H J K	/eɪ/
B C D E G P T V	/iː/
F L M N S X Z	/e/
I Y	/aɪ/
O	/əʊ/
Q U W	/uː/
R	/aː/

3 Numbers

NEW LANGUAGE	Numbers 1 to 10.
REVISION	Imperatives (for example, **Stand here please**).
MATERIALS	Flashcards of the numbers 1 to 10, written as words.
PREPARATION	Make the flashcards. Have ready ten pins or pieces of sticky tape to fix the flashcards to learners' backs.
TIME GUIDE	40 minutes.

Creating a context

1 Put this arrangement of numbered dots on the board and ask the learners to copy it.

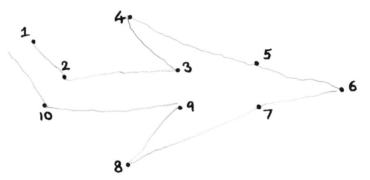

2 Point to number 1 in the arrangement of dots. Then give instructions like this:

Take a pencil. Join one and two. [*demonstrate*] Now join two and three. That's right. Now three and four. OK, now four and five. … etc.

When the learners have joined all the dots on their copies, ask them to tell you what the picture is.

3 Point to each number in turn and ask the class to repeat it.

Focus on form

4 Write the numbers one to ten as both figures and words on the board, for example:

1 one

2 two

3 three

5 Practise saying them with the learners.

6 Rub the numbers and the picture off the board.

Checking comprehension	**7** Hold up the flashcards in random order and ask the class to tell you the numbers.

8 Call ten learners to the front and ask them to stand in a line with their backs to the class. Fix a flashcard to each one's back.

9 Get the class to arrange the learners in the order of the numbers by asking them questions, for example:

TEACHER *Who is number one?*
LEARNERS *Maria.*
TEACHER *OK, Maria you are number one. Where should Maria stand? Here? OK, here. Maria, stand here please. Good. Now, who is number two?*

10 Repeat with another group of ten learners.

Pronunciation point

■ Practise /θ/ in 'three'. Teach the learners to make this sound by putting their tongue between their teeth and breathing out.

Comment

This technique can be used to present other sequences of numbers, for example 11 to 20, 21 to 30, etc. It is best to present no more than ten numbers in one lesson.

4 Telling the time

NEW LANGUAGE
What time is it?
It's _____ o'clock.

REVISION
Numbers 1 to 12.

MATERIALS
Clock face with moveable hands; nine flashcards, each with one of the following words or punctuation marks on it:

PREPARATION
Make the flashcards. Have ready ten pins or pieces of sticky tape to fix the flashcards to learners' backs. Practise miming the everyday actions.

TIME GUIDE
30 minutes.

Creating a context

1 Hold up the clock face. Move the hands to different hour positions. Tell the class the time, and something you do at that time each day. Mime the actions, for example:

> [*move the hands to 7 o'clock*] It's seven o'clock. [*mime getting up*] I get up at seven o'clock.

> [*move the hands to 12 o'clock*] It's twelve o'clock. [*mime eating*] I have lunch at twelve o'clock.

2 Move the hands to a new hour position and ask the learners 'What time is it?' Get them to answer 'It's _____ o'clock'.

3 Repeat this with several different hour positions. Work on pronunciation at this stage.

Checking comprehension

4 Mime some everyday actions (for example, getting up, having breakfast, watching television). Ask the learners 'What time is it?' When they reply, move the hands of the clock to that time.

5 Ask volunteers to come to the front of the class and mime actions. After each mime, get them to ask another learner 'What time is it?' Move the hands of the clock to that time.

Focus on form

6 Write the dialogue in speech bubbles on the board.

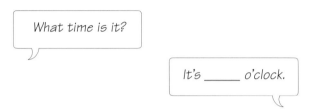

What time is it?

It's _____ o'clock.

7 Ask nine learners to come to the front of the class. Pin the flashcards you have made to their backs. Tell them to make a question and an answer by reading each other's backs and standing in the right order. The rest of the class can help!

Pronunciation points

■ 'O'clock' is pronounced /əklɒk/.
■ Practise falling intonation in question-word questions:

What time is it?

Comments

When the learners know the numbers 1 to 30, this technique can be used to teach 'It's a quarter past/half past/a quarter to' and 'It's five/ten/twenty/twenty-five past/to', etc. in the same way.

If you have no clock face available, write the different times on the board as if they were shown on a digital clock, for example '10:00'.

5 Personal information

NEW LANGUAGE   **What's your name/address?**
How do you spell that?
How old are you?
Where are you from?

REVISION   Numbers, alphabet.

MATERIALS   Form copied twice on the board; folded card saying 'Reception'.

PREPARATION   Make the 'Reception' sign.

TIME GUIDE   40 minutes.

Creating a context

1 Copy this form twice on the board:

NAME ....

AGE ....

ADDRESS ....

....

PLACE OF BIRTH ....

2 If possible, get a colleague, or a learner from a more advanced class, to join you for the first few minutes of the lesson. Put the card saying 'Reception' on your desk. Hold the chalk and look official! Ask your helper the following questions:

What's your name? How do you spell that?
[*fill in the name on one of the forms*]

How old are you?
[*fill in*]

What's your address?
[*fill in*]

Where are you from?
[*fill in*]

If it is difficult for you to find a helper, pretend someone is giving you this information on the telephone.

Checking comprehension	3	Ask a learner to answer the questions about him or herself. Fill in the second form as he or she replies. If necessary, remodel the learner's answers. Rub out the information and repeat with other learners.

Focus on form	4	Write the questions on the board and get the class and then individual learners to repeat them. Work on pronunciation at this stage.
	5	Get a volunteer to come to the front and ask other learners the questions. Tell the volunteer to fill in the form as the other learner replies. Repeat with other volunteers.

Pronunciation points

■ Practise /h/ in 'how'. Teach the learners to make this sound by pretending to laugh (Ha! Ha!) while holding a sheet of paper in front of their mouths. The paper should move.

■ Practise falling intonation in question-word questions:

What's your name?

How do you spell that?

■ Practise the stress patterns in the following sentences:

What's your name? How do you spell that?

How old are you?

What's your address?

Where are you from?

6 Countries

NEW LANGUAGE	'Countries' vocabulary area (for example, **England**, **Russia**, **Spain**).
	Where's _____ from? He's/she's from _____. Where are _____ and _____ from? They're from _____.
REVISION	None.
MATERIALS	Large map of the world; flashcards of people from about 8 different countries (some flashcards should show 2 people).
PREPARATION	Make the flashcards.
TIME GUIDE	40 minutes.

Creating a context

1   Put up the map of the world. If your learners all come from one country, ask the class 'Where are we from?'. If there are different nationalities in the class, ask individual learners 'Where are you from?'. Repeat the answers: 'That's right. We're from _____' or 'You're from _____.'

2   Ask learners to come up and point to the countries they're from on the map.

Checking comprehension

3   Put up the flashcards.

4   Introduce the people on the flashcards. Get the learners to guess where they come from, remodelling pronunciation when necessary, for example:

TEACHER   *This is Sue. Who can tell me, where's Sue from?*
LEARNERS   *Eng-er-land.*
TEACHER   *That's right. She's from England. Can you say England? Eng-land … England.*
LEARNERS   *England. … She's from England.*

Focus on form

5   Write the names of the countries on the board. Get the learners to repeat them in chorus and then individually. Make sure they can pronounce them correctly.

6   Write the questions and answers in speech bubbles on the board:

> Where's _____ from?

> He's from _____.

> Where's _____ from?

> She's from _____.

> Where are _____ and _____ from?

> They're from _____.

7   Get the learners to work in closed pairs, asking each other where the people on the flashcards are from, for example 'Where are Tanya and Boris from?' 'They're from Russia.'

Pronunciation points

▪   Make sure the learners know where the stress falls in the names of the countries:

    •
   America

     •
   Australia

   •
   England

  •
  Italy

    •
   Japan

   •
   Mexico

 •
 Russia

Comment

The countries shown here are examples. If you feel other countries are of more interest to your learners, substitute them for the examples given.

7 Nationalities

NEW LANGUAGE   'Nationalities' vocabulary area (for example, **Japanese**, **Egyptian**, **Greek**).

Is he/she _____?
Yes, he/she is.
No, he/she isn't.
Are they _____?
Yes, they are.
No, they aren't.

REVISION   'Countries' vocabulary area.
Where is/are _____ from?
He's/she's/they're from _____.

MATERIALS   Flashcards of people from different countries (see activity 6).

PREPARATION   You could make some additional flashcards.

TIME GUIDE   30 minutes.

Creating a context

1   Put up the flashcards.

2   Revise the countries you taught in activity 6, and introduce the words for nationalities, for example:

TEACHER   *This is Kyoko. Where's Kyoko from?*
LEARNERS   *She's from … Japan.*
TEACHER   *Yes, good, Japan. Kyoko's from Japan. She's Japanese. Say 'Japanese'.*
LEARNERS   *Japanese.*
TEACHER   *Good.*

3   If the class are confident, add some additional countries and nationalities.

Focus on form

4   Write the nationalities of the people on the flashcards on the board. Get the learners to repeat them in chorus. Work on pronunciation at this stage.

5   Write speech bubbles on the board:

> Is he/she _____?

> Yes, he/she is.

> No, he/she isn't.

Are they _____?

Yes, they are.

No, they aren't.

Checking comprehension **6** Ask a volunteer to come to the front of the class. Get him or her to choose a flashcard. Ask the volunteer to show the flashcard to the class, but not to you. Try to guess the nationality. Repeat with one or two other volunteers.

7 Choose some flashcards yourself. Don't show them to the class. Get the class to guess the nationalities in the same way.

Pronunciation points
- Practise /ə/ (not /æ/) in 'African', 'Australian', 'Indian', 'Italian'.
- Sometimes the stress falls on the same syllable in country and nationality words, for example:

Africa, African

America, American

India, Indian

... and sometimes on a different syllable, for example:

Egypt, Egyptian

Italy, Italian

- Practise rising intonation in yes/no questions:

Is she Greek?

Are they Australian?

8 Locating objects

NEW LANGUAGE	**Where's my _____?** **It's on the _____ / in front of the _____,** etc.
REVISION	'Everyday objects' and 'classroom furniture' vocabulary areas.
MATERIALS	About 7 everyday objects.
PREPARATION	Before the lesson, place the objects around the classroom.
TIME GUIDE	30 minutes.

Creating a context

1 Pretend to the class that you have lost the objects you placed around the room before the lesson. Look worried. For example ask 'Where's my book?' while looking anxiously around the room. Remodel the learners' answers where necessary, for example:

TEACHER *I've lost a book. Where's my book? Can anyone see my book?*
LEARNERS *Table, table! Book—table!*
TEACHER *Oh yes, it's on the the table.*

2 Repeat for the other objects.

Focus on form

3 Write the names of the objects on the board. Make sure the learners can pronounce them correctly.

4 Write the prepositions you are introducing on the board. Draw simple diagrams to illustrate them, for example:

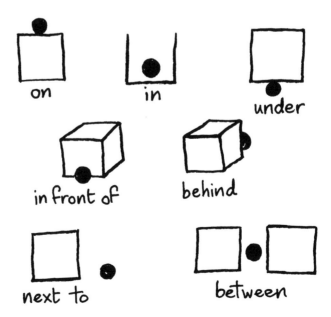

Checking comprehension **5** Ask questions about the objects you have 'lost', for example 'Where's my pen?', remodelling the learners' answers when necessary. Work on pronunciation at this stage.

6 Collect the objects. Divide the class into two teams, A and B. Get them all to close their eyes. No peeping! Put the objects in new places around the room. Get the learners to open their eyes. Ask questions like 'Where's my bag?' The first team to answer correctly gets a point.

7 The team that wins can then put the objects in new places while the others close their eyes. The winning team should ask the questions and the others should answer.

Pronunciation points ▪ Practise the stress patterns in the replies to the questions:

It's on the table.

It's in front of the cupboard.

9 Feelings

NEW LANGUAGE	'Feelings' vocabulary area (for example, **hungry**, **happy**, **sad**).

Are you _____?
Yes, I am.
No, I'm not. I'm _____.
Is he/she/(name) _____?
Yes, he/she is.
No, he/she isn't. He/she's _____.

REVISION	None.
MATERIALS	8 flashcards of faces showing different feelings.
PREPARATION	Make the flashcards. Practise the mimes for the feelings.
TIME GUIDE	30 minutes.

Creating a context

1 Put up the flashcards, one by one, telling the learners about each face as you do so, for example 'He's hot', 'She's sad'.

2 Get the learners to give each of the faces a name. Write the names by the faces.

3 Ask the learners questions about the faces, for example 'Is Peter hungry?' or 'Is Sam sad?' Get them to answer 'Yes, he is' or 'No, he isn't. He's hot.'

Focus on form

4 Write the feelings you are teaching in the middle of the board, for example:

hot

cold

hungry, etc.

Get the learners to repeat them in chorus. Work on pronunciation at this stage.

5 Turn the list into a substitution table like this:

Are you   hot?
Is he/she   cold?
*   hungry?*

Add the answers:

Yes,   I   am.
*   he/she   is.*

No,   I'm not.   I'm _____.
*   he/she isn't. He/she's _____.*

Checking comprehension 6 Mime 'cold' to the class. Encourage them to ask 'Are you cold?' Reply 'Yes, I am.' Mime other feelings and get learners to ask about them. Reply 'Yes, I am' or 'No, I'm not, I'm _____' as appropriate.

7 Ask volunteers to mime feelings to the class. Other learners should ask how he or she feels.

Pronunciation points

▪ Many learners confuse /æ/ as in 'angry' and /ʌ/ as in 'hungry'. Teach them the difference between these sounds. Get them to make /æ/ first with their mouths open. Then get them to round their lips and put their tougues back for /ʌ/. Make sure they put the /h/ sound at the beginning of **hungry** (but not at the beginning of **angry**!)

▪ Practise rising intonation in yes/no questions:

Are you tired?

Is she hungry?

10 Families

NEW LANGUAGE	'Families' vocabulary area (for example, **mother**, **father**, **sister**).
	How many _____ s have you got?
	I've got _____ _____/s.
REVISION	Numbers.
	His/her name is _____.
MATERIALS	Drawing of your family tree on the board, or on a poster.
PREPARATION	Make the poster, if you are using one, or make a sketch for a board drawing. Spend a little time preparing what you're going to say about each member of your family.
TIME GUIDE	40 minutes.

Creating a context

1 Tell the class that you are going to tell them about your family in English. If they know something about you, it may be easier for them to understand what you are going to say, but it doesn't matter if the information is new to them.

2 Put up the poster, or copy your family tree on the board. Here is an example.

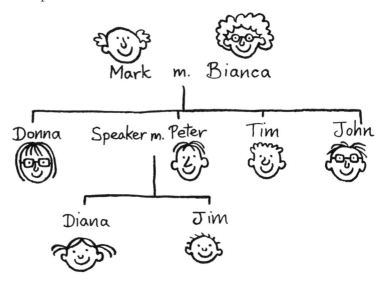

3 Introduce each family member and say a little about them, for example:

> This is my mother. Her name is Bianca. She's fifty-five now …
> I've got one sister. Her name is Donna. She's got two cats and is a very good singer.

The extra information is not to be tested later, but helps to make the lesson more interesting and natural.

Focus on form 1

4 When you have introduced your family, write the new family words on the board. For example:

father	*brother*
mother	*sister*
husband	*son*
wife	*daughter*

Checking comprehension 5 Point to faces on the family tree and ask learners to tell you their name and their family relationship, for example 'Her name is Bianca—mother'.

Focus on form 2

6 Write these speech bubbles on the board:

How many _____s have you got?

I've got _____ _____/s.

I haven't got any _____s.

Tell the learners about numbers of brothers/sisters/children in your family, for example: 'I've got two brothers and one sister.'

Checking comprehension 7 Ask learners about their families, for example, 'How many brothers have you got, John?'

8 Get the learners to work in open pairs, asking each other questions about their families.

Pronunciation point

■ Practise /θ/ in 'father', 'mother', 'brother'. Teach the learners to make this sound by putting their tongue between their teeth and breathing out.

11 Colours

NEW LANGUAGE	'Colours' vocabulary area (for example, **red**, **green**, **grey**).
	What colour is the/my/your _____? It's _____.
REVISION	'Everyday objects' vocabulary area.
MATERIALS	Flashcards of colours (about 8); at least one object for each colour, for example a red pen and a red book. Use objects the learners know already, so that they don't get confused by too much unfamiliar vocabulary.
PREPARATION	Make the flashcards. Assemble the objects and put them on your desk.
TIME GUIDE	30 minutes.

Creating a context

1 Hold up a flashcard. Tell the learners the name of the colour in English and get them to repeat it. Fix the flashcard to the board.

2 Repeat this procedure with the other colours.

3 Ask the learners about the objects on your desk, for example:

TEACHER *What colour is the pen?*
LEARNERS *Red.*
TEACHER *Yes, it's red. What colour is your bag, Kate?*
KATE *Greyn?*
TEACHER *Nearly! Look, this is grey and this is green. [points to flashcards] What colour is your bag?*
KATE *Green!*
TEACHER *Good. Yes, It's green.*

Focus on form

4 Write up the name of the colour next to each flashcard. Get the learners to repeat them in chorus and, if necessary, work on pronunciation.

5 Put the following speech bubbles on the board:

What colour is	the	_____?
	my	
	your	

It's _____.

Checking comprehension 6 Divide the class into two teams, A and B. Ask team A to close their eyes. Get team B to ask them questions about objects in the room, for example 'What colour is the board?', 'What colour is my bag?' Team A must try to remember, keeping their eyes shut. No peeping!

7 After four or five questions, ask team B to close their eyes and get team A to ask questions.

Pronunciation point
■ Some learners have problems with /l/ in 'blue', 'yellow', and 'black', and /r/ in 'green', 'grey', and 'brown'. Teach them to make the /l/ sound by putting the tip of their tongues on the part of the mouth just behind the upper teeth and pulling it away quickly as they make the sound. For the /r/ sound their tongues should curl back and not press against the top of the mouth.

12 Shapes

NEW LANGUAGE   'Shapes' vocabulary area (for example, **thin**, **round**, **square**).

What's it like?
It's _____ and _____.
Is it _____ and _____?
Yes it is.
No it isn't. It's _____ and _____.

REVISION   Colours; question-word and yes/no questions.

MATERIALS   A selection of objects of the shapes you want to teach. Make sure you have some objects which are the same colour but different shapes. Use objects of colours the learners know already, so that they don't get confused by too much unfamiliar vocabulary.

PREPARATION   Collect the objects and arrange them on your desk.

TIME GUIDE   30 minutes.

Creating a context

1 Make sure all the learners can see the objects on your desk. Choose one, but don't look at it or touch it. Get the class to guess which object you are thinking of by describing its shape and colour, for example, 'It's round and blue.'

2 Repeat this procedure for the other objects.

Focus on form

3 Write the following substitution table on the board with simple diagrams to illustrate the shapes:

What's it like?
It's thick.
thin.
long.
short.
round.
square.

4 Get the learners to repeat the shapes in chorus. Work on pronunciation at this stage.

Checking comprehension 5 Hold up the objects and ask questions, for example:

> TEACHER *Tell me about the box, Mark. What's it like?*
> MARK *It's … ah … square …*
> TEACHER *Yes, good. It's square and …?*
> MARK *… and green.*
> TEACHER *Not green, but … Helen?*
> HELEN *Blue.*

6 In the substitution table, change 'It's' to 'Is it' and add a question mark. Add:

Yes, it is.

No, it isn't.

7 Choose one of the objects on the table but don't tell the learners which one. Get them to ask questions, for example 'Is it round and green?', 'Is it thin and red?' When one learner guesses correctly, get him or her to come to the front and choose an object as you did. The rest of the class should then ask questions.

Pronunciation points

- Practise the /θ/ sound in 'thin' and 'thick'. Teach the learners to make this sound by putting their tongues between their teeth and breathing out.
- Practise the short /ɪ/ sound in 'thin' and 'thick'. (Some learners may substitute a long /iː/ sound.) Show how the /ɪ/ sound is much shorter than /iː/, and there is no 'smiling' movement of the lips.
- Contrast falling intonation in question-word questions:

What's it like?

… and rising intonation in yes/no questions:

Is it big?

13 Parts of the body

NEW LANGUAGE	'Parts of the body' vocabulary area (for example, **head**, **shoulders**, **knees**).
	Imperative verb forms (for example, **touch**, **clap**, **stamp**).
	Left, right.
REVISION	None.
MATERIALS	The song 'Head and shoulders, knees and toes'; if possible, a guitar or other musical instrument.
PREPARATION	Practise the song.
TIME GUIDE	30 minutes.

Creating a context

1 Ask the learners to stand up. Teach them the song 'Head and shoulders, knees and toes'. Touch each part of your body as it is mentioned, and get the learners to do the same.

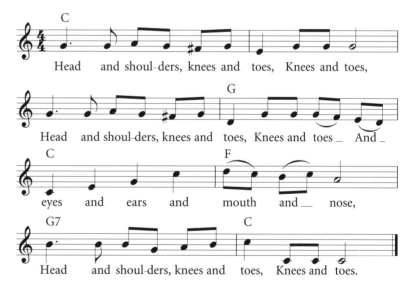

2 Present the words for 'arm', 'leg', 'hand', 'finger', and 'foot/feet' using your own body.

Focus on form

3 Write the words in a list on the board. Point to the word 'nose' and see if the learners can point to their own noses. Repeat for the other words in random order.

4 Get the learners to repeat the words. Work on pronunciation at this stage.

Checking comprehension 5   Give the learners a series of commands to perform. Start slowly. If the learners don't understand, demonstrate the action yourself. For example:

> Touch your head. Now touch your toes. Touch your nose with your right hand. [*demonstrate*] Now touch it with your left hand. That's right. Clap your hands. [*demonstrate*] Now stamp your feet. Close your eyes. Now open them again.

Give the commands faster as the learners become more confident.

Pronunciation points

- Make sure the learners pronounce 'knees' /niːz/, without the 'k'.
- In British English, the 'r' is not pronounced in 'shoulder' and 'ear'.

14 Describing people

NEW LANGUAGE	'Describing people' vocabulary area (for example, **tall, short, young**).
	What is he/she like? **He/she is _____.** **He/she has got _____ _____.**
REVISION	'Parts of the body' and 'colours' vocabulary areas.
MATERIALS	Story including descriptions of people; flashcards or board drawings of people.
PREPARATION	Make the flashcards, if you are using them. You may want to make some changes in the story below, or make up your own story.
TIME GUIDE	30 minutes.

Creating a context

1 Tell this story to the class. Put up the flashcard, or draw the picture, of each person as you talk about them.

> I'm waiting for the bus. There's a long queue today. I'm standing behind a tall thin man with short dark hair. [*put up the first picture, and use gestures to make the meaning of 'tall' and 'thin' clear*] He is smiling. In front of him is a short fat woman. She's got short fair hair and she's smiling too. [*put up the next picture and gesture to show meaning*] And so is the tall thin woman in front of her. In fact everyone in the queue is smiling! Why are they all so happy? What are they all smiling at? At the front of the queue there is one man who isn't smiling. [*put up the last picture*] Now can you tell me why are all the other people are smiling?

Focus on form

2 Write the question and the two substitution tables on the board.

What is he

she like?

He	is	tall.
She		short.
		thin.
		fat.
		small.
		young.
		old.

He	has	got	(a)	short	dark	hair.
She				long	fair	ears.
				big	curly	nose.

Checking comprehension

3 Point to individual pictures and get learners to make sentences from the tables to describe them, for example:

TEACHER *Look at this girl. What is she like? Who can help me describe her? Anna?*

ANNA *Yes. She is—um—small, and er—she is thin.*

4 Get individual learners to choose and describe a picture. The rest of the class must try and guess which one it is.

Pronunciation points

■ Practise /ʃ/ in 'short'. Teach the learners to make this sound by first making the /s/ sound (as in 'sort') and then moving the tongue back and curling up the edges to make /ʃ/.

■ Practise /θ/ in 'thin'. Teach the learners to make this sound by putting their tongues between their teeth and breathing out.

15 Clothes

NEW LANGUAGE	'Clothes' vocabulary area (for example, **trousers, shirt, dress**).
REVISION	'Families' and 'colours' vocabulary areas. Possessive forms (for example, **whose, her husband's**).
MATERIALS	Description of clothes; a bag full of clothes, a clothes-line, and clothes-pegs.
PREPARATION	Prepare your description of the clothes for stage 1. Prepare the clothes, clothes-line, and clothes-pegs. Before the lesson, fix the clothes-line across the front of the classroom.
TIME GUIDE	40 minutes.

Creating a context

1 Start to peg out the 'washing' on the line. As you do so, describe the clothes like this:

> Maria has a lot of washing today. Here are her husband's blue trousers and his white shirt. Here are her son's jeans and yellow T-shirt, and her daughter's red dress and blue blouse. This green skirt is Maria's, and so is this small white handkerchief. But whose are these bright yellow socks? ... [*look puzzled*]

Checking comprehension

2 Ask the learners questions, for example, 'Whose are the trousers?', 'Whose is the T-shirt?' Get them to answer 'Her husband's', 'Her son's', etc.

3 Do an 'oral cloze' activity. Talk to the class as you point to the items on the clothes-line, but pause before each one and encourage individual learners to call out the right word. For example:

TEACHER *Here are her husband's blue ...*
LEARNERS *... Trousers ...*
TEACHER *Good. ... And here is her daughter's red ...*
LEARNERS *Dress!*

Work on pronunciation at this stage.

Focus on form   **4**   Write the following substitution tables on the board.

Whose	is	the	white	shirt?
	are		green	skirt?
			yellow	T-shirt?
			red	dress?
			blue	blouse?
			white	handkerchief?
			blue	trousers?
				jeans?
			yellow	socks?

It's	her	husband's.
They're		son's.
		daughter's.
	hers.	

Checking comprehension 5   Ask volunteers to come to the front of the class and ask other learners about the clothes on the line. They can make sentences from the substitution tables.

Pronunciation points

- Practise the /ɜː/ sound in 'shirt', 'skirt', and 'hers'. In British English the 'r' is not pronounced in these words.
- Practise the /aʊ/ sound in 'blouse' and 'trousers'. Teach the learners to make this sound by rounding their lips, and then slowly closing their mouths.
- Practise the stress patterns in the questions and answers:

Whose are the blue trousers?

They're her husband's.

Whose is the white handkerchief?

It's hers.

16 Rooms in a flat

NEW LANGUAGE	'Rooms' vocabulary area (for example, **hall**, **living-room**, **kitchen**). This is the _____. There's a _____. There are _____ _____s. There isn't a _____. There aren't any _____s.
REVISION	'Everyday actions' vocabulary area (for example **eat**, **wash**, **watch TV**).
MATERIALS	Description of a flat; plan of the flat on a poster, or on the board.
PREPARATION	Make the poster, if you are using one. Practise the mimes in front of a mirror.
TIME GUIDE	40 minutes.

Creating a context   1   Put up the plan of a flat.

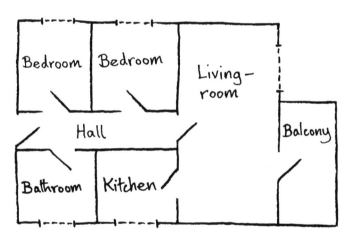

Tell the class 'This is my new flat. Come and see it!' Pretend you are showing them round, for example mime opening the door and welcoming them in.

Hello. [*open door*] Come in! Shall I show you round? Well this is the hall and, over here, this is the living-room. [*mime opening a door and walking in*] Yes, it's a nice big room, isn't it? And this is the kitchen over here. [*mime walking from the living-room to the kitchen and and opening the door*] It's quite small, but nice and modern. Of course, there aren't any stairs. The bedrooms are over here—here and here. [*mime opening doors and looking in*] And the bathroom's over here. It's a pity there isn't a garden. But there's a nice balcony out here. Look! Do you like it?

Focus on form

2   Write this substitution table on the board:

There	is	a	hall.
	isn't	two	living-room.
	are	any	kitchen.
	aren't		bedroom/s.
			bathroom.
			balcony.
			stairs.
			garden.

Checking comprehension

3   Make statements from the substitution table, some true and some false. Tell the class to call out 'Yes!' or 'No!' For example:

TEACHER   *There is a balcony.*
LEARNERS *Yes!*
TEACHER   *There aren't any bedrooms.*
LEARNERS *No!*

4   Get individual learners to tell the rest of the class one thing about their own flat or house, for example:

TEACHER   *Peter, can you tell us about your flat?*
PETER   *There is bedrooms.*
TEACHER   *How many? One? Two? Three?*
PETER   *There … are two bedrooms.*

Pronunciation points

■ Practise /ɪ/ in 'is', 'kitchen', 'living-room'. Many learners make this sound too long, like /iː/ in 'leave'. One way of emphasizing the contrast between short and long sounds is to put your hands wide apart, as if stretching a piece of elastic, for long sounds, and then bring them close together for short sounds.

■ Practise the stress in:

There's a líving-room.

There's a smáll kítchen.

There are twó bédrooms.

17 Furniture

NEW LANGUAGE   'Furniture' vocabulary area (for example, **chair**, **table**, **cupboard**).

REVISION   'Rooms' vocabulary area.
Place prepositions (for example, **near**, **beside**, **between**).

MATERIALS   Short description of a living-room; plan of the living-room on a poster, or on the board; pictures of the furniture you want to teach; if you are using a poster, pins for fixing the pictures to the poster.

PREPARATION   Make the poster, if you are using one, or do the drawing on the board. Make the pictures. Make notes for the short description of the room.

TIME GUIDE   40 minutes.

Creating a context

1   Put up the plan of the living-room.

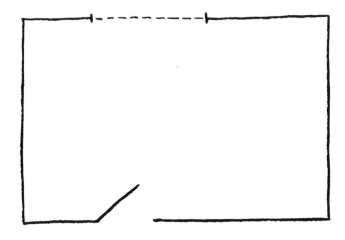 

Tell the class 'I'm moving house. This is my new living-room. It's empty now. I've got to move in all the furniture.' Show them the sofa and ask 'Where shall I put the sofa?'

Prompt them with suggestions, for example:

TEACHER   *Where shall I put the sofa? Here, by the window? Or over here, next to the door?*

LEARNERS   *Next door, next door!*

TEACHER   *Next to the door. OK. Let's put the sofa next to the door.* [pins picture to plan] *What about the armchair? Beside the sofa here? Or opposite the window, over here?*

LEARNERS   *Side of sofa.*

TEACHER   *Beside the sofa? OK.*

2 When all the furniture is in position, pretend to be on the phone to a friend telling her about the new room and how you have arranged it, for example:

> I've just moved in. The living-room's really nice. I've put the sofa next to the door. And next to the sofa there's an armchair. Oh yes, between the armchair and the sofa, there's a small round table. Opposite the armchair there's a television, and there's a rug on the floor in front of the television. I've put the picture above the television. … etc.

3 Ask a learner to come up to the board. Ask him or her to point to the pieces of furniture as you repeat your description.

Focus on form

4 Write the names of the pieces of furniture on the board. Below them, write the list of prepositions, leaving space on both sides. Get the learners to repeat the words in chorus. If necessary, practise pronunciation.

5 Make the list of prepositions into a substitution table like this:

There's a _____ near the _____.
an next to
opposite, etc.

Checking comprehension

6 Take down, or rub out, the pictures of furniture on the plan.

7 Tell the learners that they are going to work in pairs. Give each pair two pieces of paper.

8 Get one learner in each pair to copy the plan of the room onto one piece of paper. Meanwhile, the other learner should tear up the other piece of paper and write a name of a piece of furniture on each.

9 Repeat your description of the room. The learners should arrange the small pieces of paper in the right position on their plans.

10 Ask learners to make sentences to describe their rooms.

Pronunciation points

- Practise /tʃ/ in 'chair' and 'picture'. Teach the learners to make this sound by placing the tips of their tongues on the part of the mouth just behind the upper teeth (as if they were going to make a /ʃ/), and then releasing it to make a /tʃ/.
- Practise /əʊ/ in 'sofa' and /eɪ/ in 'table', showing how each of these sounds combine two different vowels.

43

18 In town

NEW LANGUAGE   'Town' vocabulary area (for example, **market**, **cinema**, **restaurant**).

On the right; on the left.

REVISION   Place prepositions.
Where's the _____?

MATERIALS   Short description of your town centre; simple plan of your town centre on a poster, or on the board.

PREPARATION   Make the poster, if you are using one. Make notes for the description of the town centre for stage 3.

TIME GUIDE   40 minutes.

Creating a context

1   Put up the poster, or draw a plan of your town centre on the board. Mark up to ten buildings and shops, but only label two or three of them. Here is an example:

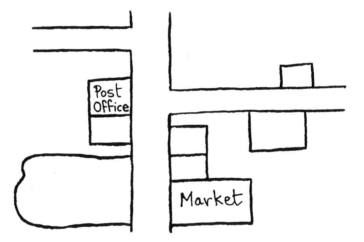

2   Tell the learners to copy your plan. While they are copying, write a list of the buildings and shops which have not been labelled on the board beside the plan. Leave spaces to the left of, and below, your list.

3   Describe the town centre to the learners, for example:

> As you walk down Queen Street, you pass the market on the right and a park on the left. Next to the market there is a baker's shop and next to that there's a butcher's. Yes, the baker's is between the market and the butcher's shop. Opposite the butcher's there's a bank. Oh yes, and the post office is next to the bank. Turn right into East Street and there's a cinema on the right and a restaurant on the left.

Point to the buildings and shops as you mention them.

Focus on form	**4**	Ask for volunteers to come to the board and write in the names of the buildings and shops which have not been labelled.
	5	Get the learners to write in the names of the buildings and shops on their own copies of the map.

Checking comprehension **6** Add the words 'Where's the' and question marks to the list of places on the board to form a substitution table, for example:

Where's	the	market?
		cinema?
		bank? etc.

Add another substitution table below with possible answers:

It's	next to	the	butcher's.
	opposite		baker's.
	behind		post office, etc.

7 Ask individual learners 'Where's the market?', etc.

8 Get learners to ask and answer questions in open pairs.

Pronunciation points

▪ Contrast the short vowel /æ/ in 'bank', 'cafe', and the long vowel /ɑː/ in 'market', 'park'. For the /æ/ sound, the mouth is open and lips pulled back as if smiling. For the /ɑː/ sound, the lips are further forward and rounded to make the longer sound, and the tongue goes down and back.

▪ Practise falling intonation in question-word questions:

Where's the bank?

▪ … and the stress patterns of the answers:

It's next to the post office.

It's opposite the cinema.

It's behind the market.

19 Directions

NEW LANGUAGE	How do I get to the _____? Go straight on. Turn right. Turn left. Take the second on the right. Take the third on the left.
REVISION	'Town' vocabulary area.
MATERIALS	Labels for buildings and shops (for example, POST OFFICE, CINEMA, BUTCHER).
PREPARATION	Make the labels by folding pieces of stiff paper so that they stand up. Write the word/s in large letters on one side.
TIME GUIDE	30 minutes.

Creating a context

1 Place the labels on various desks in the classroom and tell the learners that the classroom has become a town. Some of the desks are shops and buildings, and the spaces between the desks are streets.

2 Ask a learner to come to the front of the class. Give him or her directions. The learner should walk down the 'streets' between the desks, following your directions, for example:

> Go to the post office, please. Go straight on. … Now turn right. OK. … Now turn left. … Good. Go straight on. … Now turn right. Good. … Now you are at the post office.

Help learners to understand with gestures if they get 'lost'!

3 Repeat this exercise with a few other learners, giving directions to different places.

Focus on form

4 Write the following on the board.

Go straight on.

Turn right.

Turn left.

Take the   second   on the right.

*   third   on the left.*

5 Get the class to repeat the directions after you. Work on pronunciation if necessary.

Checking comprehension 6 Ask the class for directions to one of the labelled 'places'. Get directions from the whole class, helping them if necessary.

7 Ask individual learners for directions to two or three other places.

8 Write this speech bubble on the board above the diagrams:

How do I get to the _____?

9 Get one learner to come to the front. Tell him or her to ask another learner how to get somewhere. Repeat with two or three other learners.

Pronunciation points

▪ Practise the consonant cluster /str/ in 'street' and 'straight'. Get the learners to build up the cluster one consonant at a time, for example 'reet—treet—street' and 'raight—traight—straight'.

▪ Practise falling intonation in commands and instructions, for example:

Go straight on.

Turn left.

Take the third on the left.

20 In the market

NEW LANGUAGE   'Food' vocabulary area (for example, **apples**, **rice**, **fish**).

Yes, there's some _____.
Yes, there are some _____.
Is there any _____?
Are there any _____?
No, there isn't any _____.
No, there aren't any _____.

REVISION   None.

MATERIALS   6 to 12 food items (countable and uncountable); a shopping basket; a cloth.

PREPARATION   Prepare the food items you want to teach, a shopping basket, and a cloth.

TIME GUIDE   40 minutes.

Creating a context

1 Create a 'market' in the class by using some desks to display the food.

2 Write a 'shopping list' on the board, for example:

apples

potatoes

tomatoes

bananas

rice

sugar

fish

bread

3 Tell the class you are going shopping to buy the things on the list. Walk round the market with your basket, talking to the class about your shopping. For example:

> Potatoes—I need some potatoes. Ah—there they are. [*take some potatoes*] What's next? Apples. [*look for apples*] Oh, there aren't any apples today. … And are there any tomatoes? …

4 Make sure the things in your basket are covered so the learners have to remember what you bought. Ask questions, for example:

TEACHER   *What's in my basket? Can you remember?*
LEARNERS   *Tomatoes …*
TEACHER   *Good. Yes, there are some tomatoes. Are there any apples?*
LEARNERS   *No, no apples.*

Focus on form

5 Put these speech bubbles on the board:

> There's some _____.

> There are some _____.

> Is there any _____?

> Are there any _____?

> There isn't any _____.

> There aren't any _____.

Ask which food items from the shopping list could fill the blanks (for example 'There's some bread/rice/sugar/fish' and 'There are some apples/bananas/tomatoes/potatoes.')

6 Draw attention to 'some' and 'any'. Ask learners to try and explain, in their own language, when to use 'some' and when to use 'any'.

7 Explain the rule: 'some' in statements; 'any' in questions and negatives.

Checking comprehension 8 Put all the food back in the 'market' again.

9 Ask the learners to close their eyes, and try to remember the different items of food. Get them to tell you, using 'There's some _____' and 'There are some_____'.

10 Ask them questions about food which isn't in the market using 'Is there any _____?' and 'Are there any _____?' They should answer 'No, there isn't any _____' or 'No, there aren't any _____.'

Pronunciation point

▪ Practise falling intonation in negative statements:

No, there isn't any sugar.

21 Shopping

NEW LANGUAGE   **Have you got any __ ?**
Yes, I have.
Sorry, no I haven't.
I'd like one, two, etc. _____/s, please.

REVISION   'Containers' and 'food and drink' vocabulary areas (for example, **a bag of flour, a bottle of lemonade, a tin of soup**).
Numbers.

MATERIALS   About six different kinds of food and drink in containers (more than one container of some items, for example two bottles of lemonade, three tins of soup); a box large enough to contain at least half the items.

PREPARATION   Prepare the food and drink, and the box.

TIME GUIDE   40 minutes.

Creating a context

1   Write all the items on the board in the form of a shopping list, for example:

1 tin of peas

3 tins of soup

1 bottle of lemonade

1 bag of rice

1 jar of jam

2 packets of biscuits

2   Put all the items on your table. Check that the learners know the English words for them by holding them up and asking the class to name them. Practise pronunication at this stage.

3   If you are using six different kinds of food, ask six learners to come to your table. Turn your back and ask each learner to take one item, or group of items, and then sit down again and hide the food.

4   Turn round to face the class, and ask each of the learners for the items, one by one, for example 'Have you got any lemonade?' Prompt the replies 'Yes, I have' or 'Sorry, no I haven't'.

5   If the learner replies 'Yes, I have', ask for the number of items on your list, for example 'I'd like one bottle please' and take it. If the learner replies 'Sorry, no I haven't' continue questioning, going round the learners until you have collected all the items.

Focus on form

6 Write the following dialogue on the board:

Have you got any ___?

Sorry, no I haven't.

Have you got any ___?

Yes, I have.

I'd like   one   bottle/s   please.

two   packet/s

three tin/s

jar/s

bag/s

Checking comprehension

7 With your back to the class, so that the learners cannot see what you are doing, put some of the items in a box.

8 Call one learner to the front, and give him or her the box. He or she should be able to see what is in it, but the rest of the class should not.

9 Tell the class to 'go shopping' and ask him or her for things from the list. The learner should answer truthfully, according to whether he or she has the items or not.

10 Repeat with different learners, changing the items in the box, until the class seem confident.

Pronunciation points

■ Practise the contrast between short and long vowels in:

a tin of peas (/ɪ/ and /iː/)
a jar of jam (/ɑː/ and /æ/)

Emphasize the contrast between short and long sounds by putting your hands wide apart, as if stretching a piece of elastic, for long sounds, and then bringing them close together for short sounds.

■ Practise the stress patterns in:

I'd like two packets please.

■ Practise rising intonation in yes/no questions:

Have you got any flour?

22 Food and drink

NEW LANGUAGE	'Meals' vocabulary area (for example, **breakfast**, **lunch**, **dinner**). At _____ I have _____. What do you have for _____? I have _____.
REVISION	'Food and drink' vocabulary area; telling the time.
MATERIALS	Either examples or flashcards of common foods and drinks.
PREPARATION	Prepare the examples or flashcards of foods and drinks. If you are using flashcards, either copy some of the pictures below, adding any foods and drinks that are specific to your country, or make a collection of pictures from old magazines and food packets.
TIME GUIDE	40 minutes.

Creating a context

1 Write up the times of day main meals are usually eaten in your country. In Britain, these might be:

   7 o'clock

   1 o'clock

   6 o'clock

2 Mime eating, and then point to '7 o'clock'. Say 'At seven o'clock I have breakfast'. Do the same for 'lunch' and 'dinner'.

3 Write 'breakfast', 'lunch', and 'dinner' beside the times, like this:

   7 o'clock   breakfast

   1 o'clock   lunch

   6 o'clock   dinner

4 Display the items of food on your table, or put up the flashcards.

5   Ask the class 'What do you have for breakfast?' Encourage learners to respond with words for food and drink they know already. Introduce new words by showing the items of food on your table, or pointing to the flashcards. If learners give the word in their own language, tell them the English word and get them to repeat it.

6   Write both known and new words on the board beside 'breakfast', for example:

7 o'clock   breakfast   eggs, bread, banana, coffee

7   Do the same for 'lunch' and 'dinner'.

Focus on form   8   Write these speech bubbles on the board:

> *What do you have for   breakfast?*
> *lunch?*
> *dinner?*

> *I usually have _____.*

Checking comprehension 9   Ask individual learners to tell you what they have for different meals.

10   Get the learners to practise the dialogue in pairs.

Pronunciation points   ▪ Practise /ə/ in words like 'tomatoes', 'potato', 'banana', 'breakfast', and 'dinner'. This vowel sound is very common in unstressed syllables in English.
▪ Practise the characteristic intonation pattern in lists, for example:

I have coffee, bread, and an egg.

23 Leisure activities

NEW LANGUAGE	'Leisure activities' vocabulary area (for example, **football**, **swimming**, **reading**).
	Do you like _____? **Yes, I do. I love it.** **Not very much.** **No, I don't. I hate it.**
REVISION	Yes/no questions.
MATERIALS	Flashcards of about 8 different activities (teach activities that your learners take part in themselves).
PREPARATION	Make the flashcards.
TIME GUIDE	40 minutes.

Creating a context

1 Tell the class that you are going to show them pictures of things they do in their free time. Show the flashcards.

2 Ask learners to call out the English words for the activities if they know them (they'll almost certainly know 'football').

3 Show each flashcard again. Teach the English words the class don't know.

4 Write the words on the board, for example:

football	*going to the cinema*
swimming	*chess*
cycling	*reading*
table tennis	*sewing*

<table>
<tr><td>

Checking comprehension 1

</td><td>

5 Show one of the flashcards and ask a learner about it, for example 'Do you like football, Ben?'

</td></tr>
</table>

Focus on form

6 Put these speech bubbles on the board. Add the faces.

7 Add three more faces so that the bubbles look like this:

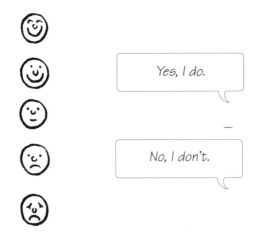

8 Teach 'Yes, I love it', 'Not very much', and 'No, I hate it', and add them beside the new faces. Practise pronunciation at this stage.

Checking comprehension 2

9 Hold up some of the flashcards again and get individual learners to say whether they love, like, or hate the activity.

10 Get the learners to ask and answer in pairs.

Pronunciation points

■ Practise /ɪŋ/ in 'swimming', 'cycling', and 'reading'. Teach the learners to make this sound through their noses.

■ 'Do you like', when spoken quickly, is pronounced /dʒəlaɪk/.

■ Contrast the pronunciation of 'do' in 'Do you like _____?' /dʒə/ (unstressed) with 'Yes, I do' /duː/ (stressed).

24 Daily routines

NEW LANGUAGE   'Everyday actions' vocabulary area (for example **get up**, **wash**, **have breakfast**).

REVISION   'Food and drink' vocabulary area; telling the time.

MATERIALS   Short description of your daily routine.

PREPARATION   Prepare a short description, with mimes, of your daily routine. Practise the mimes in front of a mirror.

TIME GUIDE   40 minutes.

Creating a context

1   Tell the learners that you are going to show them what you do on a typical day. Mime a short simple sequence of actions you carry out most days. The actions should be realistic ones that you really do and that the learners probably do as well, for example:

get up—wash—have breakfast—brush my teeth—walk to school —have lunch—go home—cook supper—watch TV—go to bed

2   Ask the learners, in pairs, to mime the same sequence to each other.

3   Describe your day, and mime the actions at the same time, for example:

Every day I get up [*mime*] at six thirty. First I wash [*mime*] and then I have breakfast [*mime*]. Then I brush my teeth [*mime*]. After that I walk to school [*mime*]. I have lunch [*mime*] at one o'clock and I go home [*mime*] at five o'clock. In the evening, I cook supper [*mime*] and then watch TV [*mime*]. I go to bed [*mime*] at ten thirty.

Focus on form

4   Write the actions in random order on the board, like this:

watch TV   *go home*

                    have lunch   *walk to school*

have breakfast   *brush my teeth*

                    cook supper

                                        get up   *wash*

          go to bed

Checking comprehension **5** Tell the story again, this time as an 'oral cloze' exercise (i.e. when you get to an action, mime it rather than using words), for example:

> Every day I [*mime 'get up'*] at six thirty. First I [*mime 'wash'*] and then I [*mime 'have breakfast'*], etc.

Tell the class to call out the words for the action each time you do a mime.

6 Write the number one beside 'get up'. Get the class to help you put all the other actions in the correct order, for example:

TEACHER *I get up and then I …?*
LEARNERS *Wash.*
TEACHER *That's right.* [writes '2' beside 'wash']

7 Ask individual learners to tell you what they do every day, remodelling their answers when necessary:

TEACHER *What do you do every day, Sam?*
SAM *I get up and … er … I wash …*
TEACHER *Good. And then? What do you do then?*
SAM *Then, I have lunch.*
TEACHER *Lunch?*
SAM *Breakfast!*

Pronunciation points ▪ Practise short vowel sounds:

> /e/ in 'bed', 'get', 'breakfast'.
> /ʌ/ in 'up', 'brush', 'lunch'.

▪ Practise /θ/ in 'teeth'. Teach the learners to make this sound by putting their tongue between their teeth and breathing out.

▪ Practise /ʃ/ in 'brush' and 'wash'. Get the learners to make the /s/ sound. Then get them to put their tongues up and back a little to make /ʃ/.

25 Jobs

NEW LANGUAGE   'Jobs' vocabulary area (for example **doctor**, **teacher**, **postman**).

What's your _____'s/ your job?
He's/ she's/ I'm a _____.

REVISION   'Families' and 'everyday actions' vocabulary areas.

MATERIALS   Short description of a family and their jobs.

PREPARATION   Prepare the short description of the family, mentioning and describing their jobs.

TIME GUIDE   50 minutes.

Creating a context   **1**   Tell the class that you are going to talk about a family and their jobs. You can either talk about your own family, or invent a family, for example:

> Today I'm going to tell you about my family and their jobs. My father is a postman. He gets up very early in the morning and makes breakfast for us all, and then goes to work to deliver the letters. My mother is a teacher. She works very hard. She teaches children in a primary school. She likes her job but she hates marking homework. … [*continue like this with four to six more jobs*]

Focus on form   **2**   Write the names of the jobs and actions you have talked about in two columns on the board. Make sure they are in jumbled order, for example:

Jobs	Actions
factory worker	teaches children
postman	types letters
farmer	cures sick people
teacher	works in the fields
businessman/woman	makes things in a factory
secretary	owns a company
doctor	delivers letters

3   Get the learners to copy the columns.

4   Repeat the description of the family. While you are speaking, get the learners to match the jobs with the actions by drawing lines between each job and its action, for example between 'postman' and 'delivers letters'.

5   Check the answers by asking volunteers to come and draw lines between the jobs and the actions on the board.

Checking comprehension 6   Ask learners 'What's your father's/mother's/brother's/sister's job?' If your learners work themselves, you can also ask 'What's your job?' If they don't know the English word for the job, teach it to them and add the job and the action to the list on the board. Work on pronunciation at this point.

7   Divide the learners into four teams for a 'jobs quiz'. Tell them about a job, for example 'He works in the fields. What's his job?' The first team to answer 'He's a farmer' gets a point. Ask a few questions yourself and then, if the learners are confident, get team 1 to ask teams 2, 3, and 4 a question, and then team 2 to ask teams 3, 4, and 1, and so on.

Pronunciation points

▪ Practise the /ə/ sound at the end of many 'jobs' words, for example: 'work**er**', 'farm**er**', 'teach**er**', 'doct**or**' (in British English the 'r' is not pronounced).

▪ Note that '-man' at the end of words like 'post**man**' and 'business**man**' is pronounced /mən/, not /mæn/.

▪ Practise the /ə/ sound, too, in the answers to questions like 'What's his job?': 'He's **a** farmer' /hiːz ə fɑːmə/.

▪ Practise falling intonation in question-word questions, and the answers:

What's his job?

He's a postman.

26 Housework

NEW LANGUAGE	'Housework' vocabulary area (for example, **make the beds, sweep the floor, do the shopping**).
REVISION	How often do you _____? Adverbs of frequency (for example, **always, usually, never**).
MATERIALS	None.
PREPARATION	Decide which housework vocabulary you are going to teach and practise the mimes.
TIME GUIDE	40 minutes.

Creating a context

1 Ask the learners, 'What do you do on Saturday mornings?' When some of them have answered, ask them 'What do you think *I* do on Saturday mornings?' They may guess. If they can't, put on a gloomy face and say 'Housework!'

2 Mime an action you want to teach (for example, 'sweep the floor') and ask the learners to guess what you are doing. Remodel their answers if necessary. Mime the other actions you want to teach and ask learners to guess in the same way.

Focus on form

3 Ask individual learners to mime actions, for example 'Peter, sweep the floor!', 'Anna, wash the dishes!'.

4 As the learners mime each action, write them in a list in the centre of the board, for example:

> *make the beds*
>
> *sweep the floor*
>
> *do the shopping*
>
> *wash the dishes*
>
> *clean the windows*
>
> *lay the table*
>
> *cook the dinner*

5 Ask the learners to repeat the list in chorus. Work on pronunciation at this stage.

6 Below the list of actions, write the frequency adverbs like this:

always   *100%*

usually

often

sometimes

never   *0%*

Point out that the frequency decreases as you go down the list.

Comprehension check

7 Ask individual learners questions like these: 'Anna, how often do you make the beds?' and 'Ben, how often do you sweep the floor?' Elicit the answers 'Always', 'Usually', 'Often', 'Sometimes', 'Never'.

8 Add the question form to the verbs you have already written up, so that you create a substitution table:

How often do you   *make the beds?*

                       sweep the floor?

                       do the shopping?, etc.

9 Get learners to ask and answer questions from the substitution table in open pairs, and then in closed pairs.

Pronunciation points

- 'Often' is usually pronounced /ɒfn/.
- Practise the /ʃ/ sound in '**sh**opping' and '**wa**sh'. Get the learners to make the /s/ sound. Then get them to put their tongues up and back a little to make /ʃ/.
- Practise the stress patterns in sentences like:

How often do you sweep the floor?

27 Abilities

NEW LANGUAGE   Yes, I can.
No, I can't. But I can _____.
Can you _____?

REVISION   'Leisure activities' vocabulary area.

MATERIALS   Flashcards of 6 to 10 leisure activities.

PREPARATION   Make the flashcards.

TIME GUIDE   30 minutes.

Creating a context

1   Tell the learners things you can and can't do. As you tell them, hold up the flashcards, for example:

I can swim [*hold up flashcard*], but I can't ride a bicycle [*hold up flashcard*].

I can dance [*hold up flashcard*], but I can't play the guitar [*hold up flashcard*].

Checking comprehension 2   Divide the class into two teams. Stand in the middle of the class and hold up a flashcard so that only one team can see it. Get this team to mime the action to the others. They must guess what it is.

3 Hold up one of the flashcards and ask a learner about it, for example:

TEACHER [holding up a flashcard] *Can you swim, Helen?*
HELEN *Yes, I can.*
TEACHER *Good. Peter, can you drive a car?*
PETER *No, I can't.*

4 Vary this by asking 'How many people can _____?' and 'How many people can't _____?' Ask learners to put their hands up and count the totals.

Focus on form

5 Write the questions and answers in speech bubbles on the board:

Can you _____ ?

Yes, I can.

No, I can't. But I can _____ .

6 Get students to ask and answer questions across the class:

JOHN *Maria, can you drive a car?*
MARIA *No, I can't. But I can ride a bicycle!*

Pronunciation points

▪ Contrast the pronunciation of the vowel in 'can' where it is /æ/, and 'can't' where, in British English, it is /ɑː/.
▪ Practise the stress patterns in questions and answers like:

Can you play the guitar?

No I can't. But I can dance.

28 Rules: 'must' and 'mustn't'

NEW LANGUAGE	**Must, mustn't.**
REVISION	'Town' and 'actions' vocabulary areas.
MATERIALS	List of public places; 2 lists of rules.
PREPARATION	Prepare the lists, or use the ones below.
TIME GUIDE	40 minutes.

Creating a context

1   Write a list of places on the left-hand side of the board, for example:

petrol station

library

school

church/mosque/temple

hospital

restaurant

prison

aeroplane

Explain any unfamiliar vocabulary.

2   Ask the learners to write the numbers 1 to 5 in their notebooks.

3   Tell the class you are going to read out five sentences. Each sentence gives rules in one of the places in the list. Tell the learners to write the name of the place beside the number in their books, for example 'hospital' beside number 1. There are eight places in the list, but only five are described, so the learners must listen carefully.

Number one. You must stay in bed and you must take your medicine.

Number two. You must pay for all the food that you eat.

Number three. You must do what the teacher tells you and you mustn't leave early!

Number four. You must turn your engine off and you mustn't smoke.

Number five. You must be quiet and you mustn't damage the books.

4 Read the sentences again and ask learners to check their answers in pairs. Then read them for a third time, pausing after each one and asking for the answer.

Focus on form   **5** In the centre of the board, write a list of things that the learners must and mustn't do at school (or work if you have adult learners), for example:

> *smoke*
>
> *run in the corridor*
>
> *arrive at 8 o'clock*
>
> *do your homework*
>
> *eat in the classroom*
>
> *listen carefully*

6 Add 'You must' and 'You mustn't' to turn the list into a substitution table, for example:

> *You must* *smoke.*
>
> *You mustn't* *run in the corridor*
>
> *arrive at 8 o'clock, etc.*

7 Get individual learners to make sentences using 'You must' or 'You mustn't' as appropriate. Practise pronunciation at this stage.

Checking comprehension   **8** Ask learners to make rules for some of the other places in your list.

Pronunciation points   ■ 'Must' is usually pronounced /məst/. It is only pronounced /mʌst/ when it is stressed. 'Mustn't' is always pronounced /mʌsnt/ (note, the first 't' is not pronounced).

■ Practise falling intonation in commands:

You must listen carefully.

You mustn't smoke.

29 Describing actions 1

NEW LANGUAGE

What is he/she/your _____ doing now?
He/She's _____ing.
What are they/your _____s doing now?
They're _____ing.
Is he/she/your _____ _____ing?
Yes, he/she is.
No, he/she isn't.
Are they/your _____s _____ing?
Yes, they are.
No, they aren't.

REVISION

'Actions', 'places', and 'family members' vocabulary areas.

Yes/no and wh- question forms.

MATERIALS

None.

PREPARATION

None.

TIME GUIDE

30 minutes.

Creating a context

1 Ask the learners to close their eyes and think of the various members of their families. Ask them questions, for example, 'What is your mother doing now?' Explain that they don't have to reply at the moment. They just have to visualize what people in their family are doing now.

Checking comprehension

2 Ask learners questions like: 'Where is your mother now?', 'What is she doing now?', 'Where are your sisters now?', 'What are they doing?' Help them with the form of the verb and pronunciation if necessary.

Focus on form

3 Write the questions and answers on the board in the form of substitution tables. Put them in speech bubbles like this:

> What is your father   doing now?
>   mother

> He is   _____ing.
> She

66

Is he _____ing?
she

Yes, he is.
No, she isn't.

What are your brothers doing now?
sisters

They're _____.

Are they _____ing?

Yes, they are.
No, aren't.

Checking comprehension 4 Get learners to ask you questions about your family using the language on the board.

5 Choose one learner and tell the others to ask him or her questions.

Pronunciation points ▪ Practise the stress patterns in questions and answers like:

Is he working?

No, he isn't. He's sleeping.

30 Describing actions 2

NEW LANGUAGE   A/the _____ is _____ing.
He /she is _____ing.
They are _____.
Who is _____ing?
What is _____ doing?

REVISION   'Actions' vocabulary area.

MATERIALS   Description of a street scene; large poster of the scene.

PREPARATION   Make the poster. Fold down the top part to hide the UFO (Unidentified Flying Object).

TIME GUIDE   40 minutes.

Creating a context

1   Fix the poster to the wall or board where the class can see it clearly. Make sure the top part is folded down.

2   Tell the class to look at the poster and listen while you describe it.

There's a busy street outside my window. Three women are standing at the bus stop and waiting for a bus. Another woman is coming out of the butcher's shop. She's carrying a heavy basket. A young man is sitting outside the cafe next to the butcher's drinking coffee. Near the cafe an old woman is selling flowers. A young woman is walking with her dog. But why is everyone looking up? What can they all see?

3 Repeat the description, and point to the people in the poster as you talk. Then ask the class 'What do you think everyone is looking at?' Ask them to guess. When they have suggested some ideas, unfold the top of the poster to reveal the UFO.

Focus on form

4 Write the following on the board:

1. Three women	is	a. walking with her dog
2. A woman	are	b. selling flowers
3. A young man		c. standing at the bus stop
4. An old woman		d. waiting for a bus
5. A young woman		e. sitting outside the cafe next to the butcher's
6. Everyone		f. carrying a heavy basket
		g. looking up
		h. coming out of the butcher's shop
		i. drinking coffee

5 Tell the class to write the numbers 1 to 6 in their books. Explain that you are going to repeat the description and they must match the sentence halves by writing one, or more, letters next to each number. Do the first one with the class so everyone understands.

6 Check the answers with the class (1-c,d; 2-f,h; 3-e,i; 4-b; 5-a; 6-g).

Checking comprehension

7 Ask the learners questions about the picture to check comprehension, for example: 'Who is selling flowers?', 'What is the young woman doing?', 'Is the young man sitting outside the cafe?'

8 When they seem confident, take the picture down and ask the class to answer from memory.

Pronunciation points

■ Practise the /ŋ/ sound in 'walking', 'selling', 'standing', etc. Teach the learners to make this sound through their noses.

69